THE S...
ST. ...ES

CYRIL NOALL

2.99

CW00338353

Gift Aid item

20 **11168340** 2811

Published by Tor Mark Press,
Islington Wharf, Penryn, Cornwall

Second edition 1989

ISBN 0-85025-303-9

© 1970, 1989 Tor Mark Press

All the photographs in this book are reproduced by courtesy of the
St Ives Camera Company, Fore Street, St Ives, from whom prints
of these and many other fine old photographs may be obtained.

Printed by Swannack, Brown & Co, Ltd., Hull

Chapter One

THE EARLY HISTORY OF ST. IVES

S T. IVES STANDS AT THE NORTH WESTERN EXTREMITY OF THE Bay of that name, on the north coast of Cornwall, about twenty miles distant from Land's End. This Bay, from Gwithian on the north-east, around by Hayle, Lelant and Carbis Bay to St. Ives itself, is fringed by a series of beautiful golden beaches, which, with the deep blue of the sea in summer, and the soft green of the grass-covered towans behind, makes a truly wonderful setting. The sheltered beaches on the Bay's western side played a great part in shaping its history. For here, in the shallow inshore waters the seine fishermen cast their nets to capture the huge shoals of pilchards which frequented these coasts during the autumn, the fish then being cured in salt and exported by sailing ship to the Mediterranean. The pilchard industry is now dead; and today the beaches are annually thronged with thousands of holidaymakers, on whom the town now virtually depends for its livelihood.

St. Ives takes its name from St. Ia, an Irish princess and missionary, who, during the fifth century, sailed over, reputedly on a leaf, and built an oratory on the site of the present Parish Church. Soon after her martyrdom at the hands of Theodoric, King of Cornwall, the small fishing village began to be called after her, the name gradually changing from Sancte Ye, Seynt Ya, Seynt Iysse, Seynt Iees, and other variants, into the modern form of St. Ives.

Until the fourteenth century the village remained an obscure place, overshadowed by its far more prosperous neighbour, the seaport of Lelant, at the head of the Bay. About that time, however, Lelant began to decline, owing to encroachment by the sands; and the trade it lost was transferred to St. Ives, which then began to grow in impor-tance. However, the inhabitants, having no building in the town where divine service could be read, were obliged every Sunday and holy day to go to Lelant church three miles distant, where their children had also to be taken to be baptised and their dead to be buried. Considering this a great hardship, they petitioned Lord Champernon, lord of St.

Inspecting the catch. Pilchard fishing was of great importance. A hewer's lookout is still to be seen at Porthminster Point

Ives, about 1408, to intercede with the Pope to licence a chapel to be built in the town. In 1410 Pope Alexander V issued his bull for this purpose; which resulted in the present parish church being begun "in the reign of King Henry V and finished in the reign of King Henry VI, being sixteen and a half years in building".

This splendid church, therefore, symbolises St. Ives' emergence as a viable township with a strongly marked community spirit. It is, however, worth remembering that the population at that time still numbered no more than about 500; so that the amount of labour and money involved in its erection must have been very considerable.

A further important advance took place in 1488, when Lord Broke, who had acquired the manor of St. Ives through marriage with the heiress of Lord Champernon, obtained a charter for a weekly Saturday market, with two annual fairs. A market house was erected in 1490, this being replaced by the present structure in 1832. Lord Broke is also credited with building the Castle for defending the town from seaward attack—a very necessary precaution in those troublesome times—some remains of which may still be seen at the landward end of the Smeaton's Pier.

In August 1497, the pretender, Perkin Warbeck, landed at St. Ives from Ireland with about 150 men. From here, he marched to St. Michael's Mount, where his lady was placed in the castle, whilst he and his followers marched to Bodmin. The attempted rebellion ended in failure, Warbeck eventually being hanged at Tyburn in November 1499.

During the reign of Edward VI the people of St. Ives joined the so-called Prayer Book Rebellion, as a protest against the introduction of the new English liturgy. The Cornishmen laid seige to Exeter, but were eventually defeated and driven back across the border. John Payne, the St. Ives Portrieve, with other leading rebels, doubtless thought to escape retribution after the collapse of their efforts; but it was not to be. Sir Anthony Kingston, the Provost Marshal, entrusted with the task of pacifying the county, was entertained by John Payne as head of the town, at the old 'George and Dragon' Inn, in the Market Place. Before dinner, Sir Anthony took the Mayor aside, and told him that an execution must be carried out that day, and asked that a pair of gallows should be erected by the time the meal was over. "The Mayor was diligent to follow this command, and no sooner was dinner ended than he demanded of the Mayor whether the work was finished.

The harbour in 1920

The Mayor answered that all was ready. 'I pray you,' said the Provost, 'bring me to the place.' The Mayor therewith took him friendly, and beholding the gallows he asked the Mayor whether he thought them to be strong enough. 'Yes,' said the Mayor, 'doubtless they are.' 'Well,' said the Provost, 'get up speedily, for they are prepared for you.' 'I hope ,' answered the Mayor, 'you mean not as you speak.' 'In faith,' said the Provost, 'there is no remedy, for you have been a busy rebel.' So presently the Mayor was hung up." The execution took place outside the Market House. A modern memorial to John Payne may be seen on the wall of the Catholic Church, at the top of Tregenna Hill. His arms—in a plain field three pineapples, doubtless a pun on his name—were carved on one of the pews of the parish church.

During the reign of Queen Mary, St. Ives was invested with the privilege of sending two members to the House of Commons. St. Ives was thus launched on a long career of notoriety as one of the rottenest of the Cornish pocket boroughs. Apart from the bribes, lavishly distributed at election times, it is doubtful if the town obtained any real advantage from the honour conferred on it; but at least the townspeople were thereby brought into contact with quite a few of the minor personalities of English history, who at various times represented them in Parliament. These included Charles Blount (1584) a Lord Lieutenant of Ireland; William Noye (1625) who, as Attorney-General, originated the levying of ship-money; Edmund Waller (1640) the poet; and Edward Bulwer-Lytton (1832), Lord Lytton, the writer.

In the sixteenth century St. Ives was very much a part of "merrie England," and this fact is plainly reflected in the customs and amusements of the people at that time. Every year, the King and Queen of the Summer Games were chosen from among the handsomest lads and lasses of the parish. Their function was to preside over the Maypole dancing and sports, all monies received being given to the poor. The Cornish Guary, or Play, was also regularly performed at St. Ives in an open air amphitheatre. These were miracle plays, the language used being Cornish, which was then still widely spoken. One amusing entry in the old Borough accounts of this time relating to these plays reads: "Spent upon the Carpenters that made Hevin, (Heaven) iiijd." Drink money for building Paradise!

In 1639 St. Ives was made a municipality, with a mayor, recorder and town clerk, plus a corporation of twelve aldermen and twenty-four burgesses. Thomas Stevens, the last of the Portrieves, was superseded as the first mayor by Richard Hext. To commemorate this event, Sir Francis Bassett, of Tehidy, who had close business connections with St. Ives, and who obtained the charter for the town, presented a beautiful silver loving-cup to the Corporation, which is still one of the town's most prized possessions, On the underside of its base appears the following inscription:

Iff any discord twixt my frends arise
Within the Burrough of Beloved St. Ives
Itt is desyred that this my Cupp of Loue
To Eurie one a Peace maker may Proue
Then am I Blest to have giuen a Legacie
So like my hartt unto Posteritie.

FCIS BASSETT ANO 1640

Two silver maces, now somewhat battered from rough usage, were provided in 1641. The Corporation's oldest surviving seal is a circular one, bearing the legend *Sigillum Burgi St. Ives in Com: Cornub: 1690.* The centre is filled with a shield, charged with an ivy-branch over-spreading the whole field; this device is a crude pun on the name *Ives*. Arising from this is the very old canard about the Mayor of St. Ives being *like an owl in an ivy bush*.

During the early part of the seventeenth century, St. Ives came increasingly under the dominance of the Puritans, and in the Civil War it was one of the only two boroughs in Cornwall which opted for the Parliamentary side, the county as a whole being strongly Royalist. In 1644 the Puritans there with their neighbours from Towednack and Zennor, assembled on Longstone Downs to the number of about 200; but when Sir Richard Grenville marched against them with 600 horse and foot soldiers the St. Ives men scattered and fled, only about three or four on both sides being killed. The Royalists then entered the town, and Sir Richard Grenville fined the Mayor (Edward Hammond) £500 for not keeping his rebellious townspeople in order. This was an enormous sum for those times; and when Hammond refused to pay he was committed to Launceston gaol, where, after three months' incarceration, he was released by order of Prince Charles. Before leaving the town, Sir Richard ordered Phillips, a Zennor constable, to be hanged, and afterwards hanged a St. Ives man at Helston and another at Truro. Capt. Francis Arundell, who had led the local forces, was proclaimed a traitor; but he escaped by sea to Bridgwater, and there joined the Parliamentary army under Fairfax. The

St. Ives men had a more successful encounter with another Royalist force, under Col. Goring. They blocked the roads with pilchard hogsheads filled with sand and made such a determined stand behind them that the Colonel and his men were checked in their march on the town and retired to Penzance.

In 1647, St. Ives was visited by the plague, during which about a third of the inhabitants died. Half of the people fled from the town, the markets were closed, and the farmers being afraid to come in with provisions, supplies were left beside the streams at Pulmanter and

Carbis Valley with prices affixed. The inhabitants later took the food away, leaving their money in payment in the water. At a critical juncture, when the town was threatened by famine, a vessel belonging to Mr. Opye, of Plymouth, unexpectedly came into the harbour laden with wheat and some butts of sack. The Mayor and Corporation purchased the cargo for £196, distributed the wheat free, and sold the wine at twelve pence per quart.

A feature of religious life at St. Ives during the following century was the growth of the Methodist movement. A Methodist Society already existed at St. Ives as early as 1743, and the brothers Charles and John Wesley both came here to assist the spread of the movement. Charles was the first to arrive, but he encountered bitter opposition from the local fishermen and miners, who attacked the meeting house, ripped out the seats and smashed the windows. John Wesley first came to St. Ives on August 30 1743. The Society then numbered about 120. "As we were going to church at eleven, a large company in the market-place welcomed us with a loud huzza; wit as harmless as the ditty sung under my window (composed, one assured me, by a gentlewoman of their *own* town),

> 'Charles Wesley is come to town,
> To try if he can pull the churches down.'

In the evening, after preaching, many began to be turbulent; but John Nelson"—Wesley's travelling companion—"went into the midst of them, spoke a little to the loudest, who answered not again, but went quietly away."

Following visits to Zennor and Scilly, John Wesley returned to St. Ives on September 16th: "In the evening, as I was preaching at St. Ives, Satan began to fight for his kingdom. The mob of the town burst into the room, and created much disturbance; roaring and striking those that stood in their way, as though Legion himself possessed them. I would fain have persuaded our people to stand still; but the zeal of some, and the fears of others, had no ears; so that, finding the uproar increase, I went into the midst, and brought the head of the mob up with me to the desk. I received but one blow on the side of the head, after which we reasoned the case, till he grew milder and milder, and at length undertook to quiet his companions."

Wesley visited St. Ives again in April 1744. On the 3rd, when leaving the house of John Nance, a leading local Methodist, in Street-an-Garrow, a few stones were thrown at him. On the 5th, "I took a view

Barnoon Hill

of the ruins of the house which the mob had pulled down a little before, for joy that Admiral Matthews had beat the Spaniards. Such is the Cornish method of thanksgiving." The Methodists at this time were unjustly suspected of sympathising with the Pope and the Pretender; and after the local vicar had preached a sermon vehemently attacking "the *new sect*, as enemies of the church, Jacobites, Papists, and what not," there were considerable disturbances, the Mayor being obliged to read the Riot Act. By 1745, however, there had been a great alteration in public feeling, so that Wesley was able to describe St. Ives as "the most still and honourable post (so are the times changed) which we have in Cornwall." The chapel in which John Wesley preached during his later visits to St. Ives still stands in Street-an-Garrow, opposite the site of the house where John Nance lived.

Chapter Two

THE STORY OF THE HARBOUR

L IFE AT ST. IVES HAS TRADITIONALLY REVOLVED AROUND ITS harbour. Here, up to about the time of the first World War, were to be seen the town's large fleets of mackerel and pilchard luggers, coasting vessels loading or discharging cargoes, seine boats arriving from Porthminster deeply laden with silvery fish; and all the bustle and activity associated with a prosperous seaport and fishing town. Today, the scene has vastly changed, yet the harbour remains the focal point of St. Ives. Nearly all the fishing boats have gone, their places taken by gaily painted pleasure craft, whilst the sand, once grimy with coal, is now a clean golden bathing beach. Many regret the change, but it was inevitable with the decline in the fishing industry; and St. Ives is at least fortunate in having a type of harbour that has adapted so well to meet new circumstances.

As early as the sixteenth century St. Ives was the chief port of departure in the west for passage to Ireland, and there are several entries in the old Borough Accounts relating to this traffic. Thus in 1592: "paide William Ots to pay for 2 passengers bounde to Irelande whiche weare hosted at water treweks 3s. 4d." "Paide to a man of Irelande that had his barke stollen by pirats 1s." 1604: "paide to a poore souldier that came from Irelande 3d." The importance of this sea-link with Ireland is shown also in a by-law passed in 1619, which decreed that "All yrishmen landing hencfforth ther loades or Burden of tymber [are to pay] ijs ijd & ballaste of Sand to be taken at this charge if they liste to take it."

No contemporary description of the harbour has survived, but it is known that prior to 1766 the pier ran out from Carn Glaze (the site of the present Fishermen's Co-operative Stores). It appears to have been of simple construction, probably consisting of timber piles driven in the sand, with a rubble filling. The maintenance of this pier and the clearance of sand from the harbour imposed at times a severe strain on the very limited borough finances.

The harbour began to take on something of its present appearance

The bottom of Fore Street, now considerably changed

in 1770, when a new pier to the design of John Smeaton, the great civil engineer, was constructed. This was built out from the Castle Rocks, the old pier being at the same time demolished and the Wharf constructed. Though only about half its present length, Smeaton's Pier sheltered a much greater extent of water than its predecessor, and so accommodated the growing trade and fishing industry of the town. This growth in the years following the building of the pier is best illustrated by the annual amounts of harbour dues collected by the Trustees which rose from £593 in 1770 to £1,280 in 1814 and to £1,824 1s. by 1836. In 1837 St. Ives, very unwisely, was declared a free port, and dues ceased to be collected—a measure that resulted in unavoidable delay in carrying out further improvements.

In 1844, 165 coasting merchant vessels having a gross tonnage of 9,723 arrived in the port of St. Ives. By comparison, during the same year, 856 vessels arrived at Hayle, these having a tonnage of 65,979. But what was more important at St. Ives was the fishing industry; in 1847 the capital invested in the pilchard fisheries was in excess of £150,000, with 400 boats and 735 men employed, whilst a further 100 men were engaged in other types of fishing. Imports, coastwise, were, coal, iron and general merchandise; foreign, timber: exports, coastwise, fish and copper ore; foreign, fish and tin. Sailing vessels belonging to the port totalled 8,994 tons, with a few steamers totalling 498 tons.

In 1864 work was begun on an outer harbour by erecting the New or Wood Pier at the seaward side of Smeaton's structure, and running roughly at right angles to it. Its timber frame failed to stand up to the buffeting of the Atlantic rollers, however, and in less than twenty years it had become an almost complete wreck; today little more than its short masonry stump remains. The failure of this project brought on an acute crisis, the harbour being desperately overcrowded with the ever-increasing fleet of fishing vessels. This situation reached its climax in 1886, with the so-called Tresidder's riot among the fishermen. Eventually, in 1888-90 the position was relieved by adding a lengthy extension to Smeaton's Pier. The shorter West Pier was built in 1894 as a loading jetty for roadstone from the Carthew and Orange Lane quarries. Finally, around the year 1922 the Wharf Road was constructed from the lifeboat house to Chy-an-Chy, affording much needed relief to Fore Street, which previously had to carry all the traffic.

In the half century that has followed since then, St. Ives has ceased to be a seaport, whilst its fishing fleet has dwindled almost to extinction.

The crowded harbour in the days of sail

These events have brought about great changes in the town itself. The smoke houses, for curing kippers, the great pilchard cellars, the barking houses for tanning nets, and the net factory have all gone, either swept away to make room for modern developments, or converted to new uses. The last St. Ives pilchard cellar, in Norway Lane, was cleared out in 1968-69, much of its equipment being transferred to the St. Ives Museum, at Wheal Dream. Yet, with all these changes, "Downlong," the old fishing quarter, still retains a great deal of its atmosphere, the narrow alleyways and picturesque cottages proving a never-failing delight to artists, photographers and holiday-makers.

Chapter Three

WHAT TO SEE

FOR THE AVERAGE HOLIDAYMAKER, ST. IVES' GREATEST attraction probably lies in its superb beaches, varying in character from exhilarating Porthmeor, on the north of the town, where surf riding may be enjoyed, to the safer "family" beaches of Porthgwidden, Porthminster and Carbis Bay, and the solitude of Porthkidney. But there is much more to enjoy at St. Ives than mere sand for the old town itself is full of history and character. In former times, St. Ives was rigidly divided into two halves, known as "Uplong" and "Downlong", the Market House forming the watershed between them. "Downlong" comprised the fishing community, whilst the tradesmen, sea captains and professional classes lived "Uplong". A different order of things prevails today; but the two parts still preserve much of their old identities.

A large part of "Downlong" is built on what was originally a sandbank lying between the harbour and Porthmeor, and connecting the grass-covered headland called the Island with the "mainland". The Island it may be added did once justify its name, but that was long before the town's recorded history began. This part is a maze of little streets, passages and courtyards, bearing such quaint names as the Digey, Bethesda Place, Mount Zion, Love Lane, Teetotal Street, and Harry's Court. In the Digey (which connects Fore Street with Porthmeor) may be seen an old stone arch, which formed the entrance gateway to the mansion of the Hicks family. The house, which was an interesting one, has now virtually disappeared, but the arch and the name "Hicks' Court" perpetuate its memory.

In Victoria Road stands a curious old house built upon a rock. Now divided in two, it was once a public house known as "The Labour in Vain". This curious title was explained by its signboard, which showed a woman vainly endeavouring to scrub a little negro boy white. The child is said to have been the survivor of a ship lost at Porthmeor, and brought to this house—then the nearest to that beach— where the good lady set to work on him briskly with soap and water.

The harbour front contains several interesting features. Here, for instance, may be seen St. Ives' two lifeboats. The main lifeboat, named *Frank Penfold Marshall*, is drawn from its house near the West Pier by tractor along Wharf Road and launched into the harbour at Chy-an-Chy. The smaller I.R.B. (inshore rescue boat) is separately housed in the harbour car park. The St. Ives station has achieved a magnificent record of service since its establishment in 1840. A shocking lifeboat tragedy occurred here on January 23 1939, when the *John and Sarah Eliza Stych* capsized three times in a terrible storm going to the assistance of an unknown vessel. The boat was finally wrecked at Gwithian with the loss of seven out of eight members of her crew.

Along the harbour will be found the fishermen's lodges, Shamrock, Shore and Rose View: a fourth, Bay View, was hit by a storm some years ago. Visitors are always welcome in these places, where interesting conversations may sometimes be had with the old salts. A pleasant custom is observed of flying bunting to celebrate the wedding of a member of the old fishing community, and the hoisting of a flag at half mast when one of them dies.

Several ancient inns, much frequented by sailors, once existed in the harbour. Only one of these—the celebrated "Sloop", a picturesque

overleaf: the harbour in the twenties

building of considerable antiquity—is still licensed today, the others being the "Globe," the "White Hart" and the "Ship Aground", all now in use as shops. In front of the old "Globe" runs a low wall, built by one licensee named Doble, to keep the sea from entering the ground floor at high spring tides. The young fishermen, however, found this wall a comfortable seat, and in an effort to get rid of them, Doble reduced the wall to half its original height—but this only made it more comfortable than ever! It has remained ever since a popular gossiping seat, and its name, "Doble's Wall", has entered local folklore.

At the landward end of Smeaton's Pier stands the medieval fishermen's chapel, dedicated to St. Leonard. Here, according to a writer in 1808, "prayers were formerly read to the fishermen before they went to sea, to beg success on their undertaking, by a friar who was stationary here. The congregations are said to have paid him for his trouble, with a part of their fish, when they returned. The form appeared to us to be even now kept up by a poor fanatic, whom we found addressing this incorrigible race of men upon the Quay. His congregation, however, did not appear to be very attentive to him, nor could we wonder at his eloquence being thrown away upon them, when we learnt that he was generally *drunk*, and, at his intervals of inebriety, always *mad*." During the building of Smeaton's Pier this ancient sanctuary served as a blacksmith's shop, and it has since been used by fishermen as a shelter in stormy weather. In recent years a bronze memorial was set up in the chapel recording the names of local men drowned at sea.

Another chapel much used by former fishermen is situated near Chy-an-Chy, at the bottom of Fore Street. Formerly the Primitive Methodist Chapel, it was built in 1831. Blue elvan "bowlies" (sea-rounded rocks) used during its construction were brought to the harbour by fishing boat from Porthmeor Cove, near Gurnard's Head, and women are said to have carried them in their aprons up the beach to the building site. This chapel has achieved world-wide celebrity owing to its association with three famous pictures, painted towards the end of last century by W. H. Y. Titcomb. Two of them—*Primitive Methodists at Prayer* and *A Mariner's Sunday School*—depict scenes within the chapel itself; whilst in these and in *Piloting Her Home*, many of the "character" parts were taken by members of the congregation.

The sailors also had their chapel at St. Ives, on the summit of the Island, and dedicated to St. Nicholas. Leland wrote of it in 1538:

January 1908. The wreck of the coasting schooner *Lizzie R Wilce*, which subsequently broke up. In the background is another schooner, *Mary Barrow*, which was refloated

"There is now at the very point of Pendinas"—the old Cornish name for this headland—"a chapel of St. Nicholas and a pharos for lighte for shippes sailing by night in these quarters." The town authorities were responsible for its upkeep. In 1593 we find "paid to John Kalamey ffor mending St. nicholas Chapell, 1s. 4d." In later years it became a look-out for the preventive men and pilots, and eventually passed into the hands of the War Office, who used it as a store. In 1904, having no further use for the building, and being ignorant of its antiquity,

they began to pull it down. The result was a local outcry, and the work of destruction was stayed. In 1911, the St. Ives shipowner, Sir Edward Hain, restored the building to commemorate the Coronation of King George V. Originally, the chapel perched picturesquely amidst the rocks, but it is now surrounded by an artificial-looking platform.

At the opposite end of the Island are the remains of a battery erected during the last century for the defence of the town. This promontory for long played an important role in local defences, as its Cornish name, mentioned by Leland — "Pendinas," the fortified headland — plainly signifies. Some traces of these older fortifications are still to be seen. The rocky bluff at the N.E. extremity of the headland is known as the Lamp Rock, there once having been here a pole with a lantern fixed on top to guide fishermen at night into Porthgwidden Cove, then the principal landing place.

Towards the harbour at Wheal Dream stands a large building, formerly the Seamen's Mission, which now accomodates the St. Ives Museum. Here are to be seen many relics of the town's old industries and crafts, local bygones and an extensive collection of pictures, including some by well-known St. Ives artists. The first curator of the museum was Cyril Noall, author of this booklet and many other books on mining and the history of Cornwall. A memorial tablet is displayed on the outside of the building. The Fore Street market has also been renamed in his memory.

At the foot of Porthmeor Hill, leading from Porthmeor Beach to Ayr, is the ancient holy well of Venton Eia (St. Eia's or Ia's well) which in olden times was held in highest reverence. It also formed one of the main supplies of drinking water, which was carried home in "patticks" (earthenware pitchers) and buckets. In 1692-3 the well was covered, faced, and floored with hewn granite blocks in two compartments, just as it will be found today.

St. Ia's well brings us naturally to the subject of the church also dedicated to this saint, whose handsome tower rises proudly above the grey slated roofs of old St. Ives. As already mentioned, this structure dates from the early part of the fifteenth century. The granite used in its construction was quarried in the parish of Zennor, about five miles distant; and owning to the absence of roads in those times, had to be conveyed to St. Ives by sea. In spite of the havoc wrought by the Puritans, who destroyed both the "organs" and "railings"—rood screen—and by over-zealous Victorian restorers, the interior of this building still retains much of its medieval glory. Attention is particularly directed to the beautiful carved wagon roof; the fifteenth century font, with carved beasts on the base representing demons cast out by baptism; and the ancient bench-ends, whose deep cutting is typical of Cornish wood-carving of that period. Just outside the south door stands a very fine cross dating from the 15th century.

For those who enjoy walking, several interesting excursions on foot may be made from St. Ives. One of the best of these lies by way of the coastal path to Carbis Bay and Lelant. Starting at Porthminster Beach (below the railway station); this first ascends to Porthminster Point, where may still be seen the old "Baulking House", a two-storey building ,flanked on either side by look-outs; here the "huers" kept watch for pilchard shoals entering the Bay and with semaphore and trumpet directed the fishermen how best to shoot their seine net around them. Passing via the Hain Walk to Carbis Bay, the path winds around Carrack Gladden or Hawke's Point, and so reaches the celebrated Nut Grove and Wishing Well. The former—a hazel copse—runs along the cliff above Porthkidney Beach for about a quarter of a mile, and in its midst is the ancient holy well of St. Uny, patron saint of the parish of Lelant and brother to St. Ia. It consists of a stone basin fed by a small stream trickling down the cliff. To use it as a wishing well, one must drop a bent pin into the water whilst making the request, but the wish must not be revealed to anyone, or it will not be granted.

Beyond the Nut Grove lies the broad expanse of Lelant Towans, home of the West Cornwall Golf Club, with Lelant Church at its further end. This building possesses a Norman arch and several interesting memorial tablets including a particularly attractive, though damaged, slate to the Praed family, who resided at Trevetho, in this parish. One of the Trevetho Praeds—a banker—gave his name to Praed Street, in London.

Lelant is a pretty and secluded village, lying on sloping ground above the Hayle estuary, and containing a number of picturesque old cottages. The estuary is a bird sanctuary where, in winter particularly, many rare species may be seen.

Behind the village rises the flat-topped hill of Trencrom, which commands magnificent views over a large part of West Cornwall, including both St. Ives and Mount's Bays. Here was a very ancient fortress, with large stone ramparts and gateways and numerous hut circles. Two neolithic axes and fragments of Iron Age pottery have been found here, but the site has yet to be excavated. Trencrom Hill now belongs to the National Trust.

Westward from St. Ives there is a beautiful coastal walk to Clodgy and Hor Points. This skirts Porthmeor Beach and follows the cliff top to Clodgy, where there is the magnificent "Five Points" view. Visitors have been known to complain that there are only *four* points to be seen, but they forget that the fifth is Clodgy itself, on which they are standing! One may return to St. Ives by a different route, along Pednavounder Lane. The coastal footpath continues westward towards Zennor.

There is also an enjoyable walk from St. Ives through the fields and farms to Zennor. For most of the way it runs through the narrow coastal plain lying between the sea and the hills inland, and affords fine views of moorland on one hand and sea on the other. The path begins at a stileway in Burthallan Lane, and traverses many small stone-fenced fields, passing the farms of Trowan, Trevalgan, Trevegia, Trendrine, Wicca, Tregerthen and Tremeadow to Zennor Churchtown. If time permits, one may make a diversion from Wicca down to Trevail Cove, by the way of a very pretty sheltered valley where fuchsias grow wild along the river banks. From cliffs above the cove a view of the bold headland at Gurnard's Head may be obtaind, whilst just offshore lie the Western Carracks—the "Seal Island" of the St. Ives boatmen—where seals are often seen basking on the rocks. At Zennor, the unusual Wayside Museum, founded by the late Col. Hirst, is well worth a visit, whilst the church boasts a celebrated Mermaid.

Chapter Four

LOCAL FOLKLORE

CORNWALL IS RICHLY STEEPED IN FOLKLORE; AND MANY interesting stories have come from the St. Ives district. One of the most characteristic is that of "The Lady with the Lantern". This tells how, one evening, around dusk, during a year notorious for storms and wrecks, a large ship was driven on a sunken rock at the back of the Island. Many of those on board perished at once, and as each successive wave urged the wreck onward others of the crew were swept into the angry sea. Despite the terrible conditions, a boat was manned by some St. Ives fishermen and rowed towards the ship. Approaching as near as they dared, they managed to rescue two or three sailors by means of ropes. Then a group appeared on deck supporting a lady who held a child in her arms. The lady, despite entreaties, refused to give her child to the care of a sailor whilst they endeavoured to pass her across to the boat. So, with the ship fast breaking up, she was lowered into the sea, and the fishermen drew her through the waves. In her passage, the lady fainted, and was taken into the boat without the infant. The child had fallen from her arms, and was lost in the boiling waters. She later regained consciousness; but finding her child was gone, she lost hope, and died. They buried her in the churchyard; but shortly after a lady was seen to pass over the churchyard wall on to the beach and walk towards the Island. There she spent hours amid the rocks, looking for her child, before returning to her grave. When the nights were stormy or very dark, she carried a lantern, but on fine nights she made her sad search without a light. The Lady and the Lantern have ever since been regarded as predictors of disaster on this shore.

Less well known than this story, but equally authentic, is the legend of the White Horse of Porthgwidden. In the early part of the nineteenth century a gentleman called Birch owned a magnificent white horse with a flowing mane and a flying tail. The animal was beautifully groomed and the delight of his master. Every evening at dusk Birch would ride on his horse to Porthgwidden for a bathe. He was a powerful swimmer; but one stormy evening the wind and waves proved too

The model boat competition, sometimes held in the harbour, taken before 1922 when the Wharf Road was constructed

much for him, and he was swept away and drowned. Some time later the fishermen noticed the horse patiently waiting on the beach, far beyond the usual time for its master's return, and so came to learn of the tragedy which had occurred. Some time after this people living in the vicinity vowed that, after dusk, the ghost of Mr. Birch and his lovely horse was seen riding through Island Road, down to Porthgwidden Beach, and out to sea. This spectre is said to have been seen as late as the 1890's.

The pilots of St. Ives had a superstition regarding "Jack Harry's Lights," these phantoms being named after the man who was first deceived by them. They were generally observed before a gale, and the ship seen with them resembled the one which later was sure to be wrecked. Scores of pilots had seen and been led a fine chase after them. One old pilot told of how they put off in their big boat, the *Ark*, when a large vessel was reported in the offing. The vessel stood off the head, the wind blowing W.N.W. They went off four or five miles, and thought they were alongside when the ship slipped to windward a league or more. Again the *Ark* went in pursuit and once more closed in on the stranger; but away she flew to Godrevy over the course they had just sailed; so the pilots gave it up for "Jack Harry's Light", and with disappointed hopes bore up for the harbour. These manifestations may be likened to those of the *Flying Dutchman*, seen off the Cape of Good Hope.

Another superstition prevalent at St. Ives, was that known as "The Seven Whistlers". The occurrence at night of these whistling noises presaged death or misfortune to the hearer, or even disaster to the district if repeated several nights running. Sceptics attributed these sounds to flocks of migrating birds passing over by night. Certainly St. Ives fishermen believed whistling at night to be very unlucky; and an informant told one writer "I would no more dare go among a party of fishermen at night whistling a popular air, than into a den of untamed tigers".

The countryside around St. Ives has produced several enchanting fairy stories. One of the best of these comes from Lelant. A man from there was returning from the port with some pilchards one moonlit night; and *en route* he thought he heard the bell of Lelant church tolling. Upon a nearer approach he saw lights in the church, whilst he noticed that the bell made a dull heavy sound, as if muffled. He peeped in through a window, and eventually saw, by a strange all-pervading light, a funeral procession moving along the central aisle. The little people crowding the church looked very sorrowful, although they did not wear any mourning; indeed, they wore wreaths of little roses and carried branches of blossoming myrtle. Six of them bore a bier on which lay the corpse of a beautiful female, smaller than the smallest child's doll. Her body was covered with white flowers, and her hair, like gold threads, was tangled amongst the blossoms. As he watched, a party of men with picks and spades dug a hole by the altar, and into this the body was laid. As it disappeared, the mourners tore off their flowers and broke their branches of myrtle, crying, "Our queen is dead! our queen is dead!" One of the gravediggers threw a shovelful of earth upon the body; and the shriek of the fairy host so alarmed the watcher that he involuntarily joined in it. In a moment, all the lights were extinguished and the fairies flew in every direction. Many, shrieking, pierced him with tiny daggers as they passed, and he was obliged to flee to save his life.

Trencrom Hill is associated with stories of the spriggans. At the little village of Chyangweal, now part of Carbis Bay, lived the widow of a tinner who had been killed in one of the ancient "coffens" or open mine workings on Worvas Hill, above Wheal Providence. Every night the Trencrom spriggans would meet in the widow's cottage to divide their plunder, and on leaving placed a coin by her bedside as she slept, or pretended to sleep. This she considered insufficient reward for her discretion and one night put a charm upon them by putting on her shift inside out while beneath the bedclothes. The spriggans fled in terror, leaving their booty behind, whereafter the old woman moved to St. Ives, to live in luxury like a high-born lady.

One of the loveliest legends associated with this part of Cornwall is that of the Weeping Fern of Carrack Gladden. From cave entrances on this headland (which divides Carbis Bay and Porthkidney beaches) and along the stretch of cliff between there and Lelant Towans the beautiful maidenhair fern used to grow in profusion. Its fronds hung down in dense clusters, like a lady's tresses, whence arose its attractively descriptive name. The luxurious growth was due to tiny streams of water which forever trickled down the cliff among its delicate fronds and hung glistening from its extremities like teardrops. This circumstance gave rise to the legend of the two young lovers who used to walk along this shore together. On one occasion they parted for a while, she to gather flowers, he to bathe, but a treacherous current swept him

25

out to sea and he was drowned. Lying on the grassy cliff top, the young girl watched and waited for her lover, by the hour until gradually the terrible truth dawned upon her and, weeping long and bitterly, she died.

They say the maiden is still weeping there today as the droplets fall from the delicate leaves, although there are far fewer maidenhair ferns at Carrack Gladden than there were a century ago due to the vandalism of plant collectors, but it is now, fortunately, protected by law. The picturesque stone grotto which stood on the little headland adjoining the Towans has completely disappeared; but the Nut Grove and Wishing Well remain, and so, too, does much of the old enchantment of the place. Morgan Anthony, who collected the tale of the weeping fern, was a close friend of William Bottrell, the Cornish folklorist, who lived in a little cottage at Carrack Gladden. To Bottrell's industry we owe the preservation of so much of our West Cornish traditions, including that of the Mermaid of Zennor. But he somehow missed this delightful though tragic story lying, one might say, right on his own doorstep.

Chapter Five

ANCIENT CUSTOMS

ST. IVES IS FORTUNATE IN HAVING PRESERVED SEVERAL QUAINT old customs and ceremonies which are well worth the notice of he visitor. One of the most interesting is the game of hurling the silver all, which takes place every Feast Monday—that is, the first Monday fter February 3rd, the anniversary of the consecration of the Parish Church in 1434. Lelant Feast falls on February 2nd; and formerly it vas the custom for St. Ives to play Lelant, their respective parish hurches being the two "goals". Eventually the people of St. Ives utnumbered those of Lelant, making the game too one-sided. A new rrangement was then agreed upon, whereby two teams were formed y the St. Ives men, one consisting of all those bearing the Christian ames of Thomas, John or William, and the other of all those having ther names. The two sides ranged themselves on the Fore Sand, and the Mayor threw the ball from the churchyard wall, hence the old rhyme,

Toms, Wills, and Jans,
Take off all's on the san's.

A pole was set up on the beach, and each side tried to get the oftenest t the "goold," as the pole was called, their opponents manfully triving to keep them away and at as great a distance from it as possible. n latter years hurling has ceased to be played by adults, and is now onfined to the schoolchildren, who are given a holiday for the purpose. The ball is thrown by the Mayor at ten-thirty; and the child who returns : at noon receives a reward of five shillings. Pennies are also thrown o the children. The silver ball is about the size of an orange, covered vith thinly beaten silver, and bears the Cornish inscription "Guare ag yu guare wheag"—"fair play is good play". A similar game is lso still played at St. Columb, near Newquay.

On the top of Worvas Hill, which rises behind Carbis Bay and com-ands extensive views over the surrounding district, stands a three-ded granite pyramid. This was erected by John Knill, who held the mportant post of Collector of Customs at St. Ives from 1762-82 and ho was Mayor in 1767. Knill in 1797, settled upon the mayor and

launching a boat in the harbour

capital burgesses of the town an annuity of £10, to meet the expense
of a quaint little ceremony which is still held every fifth year around
this monument on St. James' Day (July 25th).

By the terms of Knill's trust deed, ten girls, not over ten years of age
natives of the borough and daughters of either seamen, fishermen or
tinners, must dance for a quarter of an hour between ten and twelve
in the morning on the ground adjoining the mausoleum, "and after
the dance sing the 100th Psalm of the old version, to the fine old tune
to which the same is sung in St. Ives Church". The girls' singing and
dancing is accompanied by a fiddler; whilst two widows of seamen
fishermen or tinners attend the ceremony, and certify to the Mayor
Collector of Customs and clergyman—who form the trustees—that
has been duly performed. Money is provided to buy white ribbons for
the girls and a cockade for the fiddler. Originally, sufficient funds were
available for a dinner for the trustees and their friends, and for various
other purposes. For example, £5 was paid to a man and his wife who
had reared to the age of ten the greatest number of legitimate children
without parochial assistance; £5 to the woman deemed to be the best
knitter of fishing nets; and £5 to the best curer and packer of pilchards
The funds also had to provide for the upkeep of the mausoleum, in
which Knill intended to be interred; however, owing to difficulties re
garding its consecration, he was in fact buried in London, where he
died, in 1811, aged 77.

Two interesting ceremonies which have been revived in recent years
are the Midsummer Eve Bonfire and "Crying the Neck". The bonfire
is lit at dusk on a hill near the town, a bunch of herbs being ritualistic
ally thrown in the flames by the Lady of the Flowers, prayers in Cornish
also being offered. Though now given a Christian veneer, this ceremony
is really a perpetuation of the old pagan Baal fires, connected with the
worship of the Sun. It is one of a chain of bonfires lit throughout the
county. "Crying the Neck" takes place at the end of harvest. A small
patch of corn left standing in a field is ceremoniously cut with a scythe
by the farmer, to the cry of "A neck, a neck! a neck!" This corn
then bound into a sheaf, whilst those attending take away a few ears
to keep till the following harvest, for good luck.

Several other interesting customs were formerly observed at St. Ives
but these unfortunately died out between the two World Wars. One
of the most colourful was the annual "Guise Dancing"—the word
guise being pronounced in the French fashion—which took place during

the twelve days of Christmas. The young people dressed themselves up in all manner of disguises, "the town being literally given up to a lawless mob, who go about yelling and hooting in an unearthly manner, in a tone between a screech and a howl, so as to render their voices as undistinguishable as their buffoon-looking dresses". Some of the performers would get up a little play about Old Father Christmas or bold King George, and go from house to house giving performances of it.

"Fairy Mo"—the ancient "pig fair"—was celebrated a few weeks before Christmas. Its main feature consisted of street stalls, or "standings," at which fruit, sweetmeats and fairings could be purchased. A general atmosphere of merrymaking prevailed, and there was a wide variety of sideshows and other entertainments. The war-time black-out restrictions in 1939 put paid to this centuries-old fair, though its name is still retained for an indoor bazaar run by the church.

On Shrove Tuesday the boys armed themselves with stones tied to cords, and paraded the town, slinging them against the doors whilst shouting,

> Give me a pancake, now—now—now,
> Or I'll souse in your door with a row—tow—tow.

May Day was also kept up by the young people with considerable spirit. Young branches of sycamore were cut to make whistles and "pee-weeps," the ease with which the wood could be slid out from the surrounding tube of bark making this an easy operation. The day was then ushered in with the blowing of these instruments, and tin "May horns". This custom died out in the 1930's. Another practice which ceased at about the same time was that of placing a special type of large apple under a child's pillow on "Allan Day"—Allhallows Eve, which was eaten with relish the following morning.

St. Ives children today, however, can still look forward each year to one time-honoured custom which remains vigorously alive—the Good Friday model-boat sailing on Consols Pond, at the top of the Stennack. This practice has a very ancient origin. In pagan times, fishermen sent miniature boats to sea at the beginning of their summer season, hoping that this offering would be accepted and their own boats spared from disaster. The only other place where this custom has been observed in recent times is Sark, in the Channel Islands.

Chapter Six

LOCAL PLACE NAMES

VISITORS TO CORNWALL ARE OFTEN INTRIGUED BY THE CURIOUS place names found throughout the county, which are quite different from those of Saxon origin in other parts of England. Such names are, in fact, the last living vestiges of the ancient Cornish language which continued to be spoken in the western part of the county until about two centuries ago.

St. Ives has its fair share of old Cornish names. All its beaches have names beginning with the prefix "porth", meaning sandy cove. Thus we have Porthmeor (big cove); Porthgwidden (white cove); Porthminster (church cove—there was anciently a little chapel here beside the stream); Porthrepta—the old name for Carbis Bay; and Porthkidney, the meanings of the last two being a little obscure. In the town itself are several street names of Cornish origin. Street-an-Garrow—rough street—no longer lives up to its reputation in these days of universal tarmac; nor does Street-an-Pol—pool street—now add its quota to the town's water supply. Where Fore Street meets the Wharf, is found Chy-an-Chy—the house by the house—probably an ancient name recalling the time when two isolated dwellings stood here side by side. The Digey has puzzled philologists, the obvious translation of "farmstead" appearing to them too inappropriate for a street in this position, yet this meaning would seem to be endorsed by the adjoining English place name of The Meadow.

The rocky bluff between Porthgwidden and Wheal Dream is known as Carn Crows, meaning cross rocks, probably indicating that an ancient Cornish cross was once set up here. The word "carn" occurs in many other names of rocks on the adjoining coast, but Carn Glaze—grey or blue rock—is actually found in St. Ives harbour, where it is still to be seen in the foundations of several houses. A revealing glimpse of how St. Ives appeared in former times is afforded by many of these old names. For example, Barnoon (Bar-an-woon) signifies the top of the down; but this down is now completely covered with terraces; whilst Parc-an-roper—the roper's field—is now a coach park.

An August Saturday afternoon when everyone travelled by train, immediately post war

Some of the English place-names of St. Ives are also curious and amusing. Take, for example, Skidden Hill. This steep thoroughfare was formerly the main approach road to the town, and drivers of heavy timber waggons had to be careful to apply their skids (brakes) when descending, hence the name. The Warren, between Westcott's Quay and Porthminster Beach, recalls the days, very long ago now, when a rabbit warren existed in this area. Several of the little streets and alleys leading off from the Wharf bear singular names. Mount Zion serves as a reminder of a long-vanished former meeting house or chapel. Bethesda Hill is even more interesting. Many years ago someone noticed that the street possessed five porches, whilst at the bottom of the hill lay a pool—the harbour. It thus fitted the description given in the New Testament to the Pool of Bethesda, within the wall of Jerusalem, where Christ healed the impotent man; and so Bethesda Hill it was christened.

Another Downlong name that never fails to attract the notice of the observant passer-by is Teetotal Street, commemorating the hold which the temperance movement gained at St. Ives during the last century. A Teetotal Society, with an associated circuit of chapels in West Cornwall, was established in the town; its main chapel was in Chapel Street, the building now serving as a drill hall. Several lanes bear names of their former principal residents. Examples are Bailey's Lane, Harry's Court, Hicks' Court, and Court Cocking. Whether Bunker's Hill belongs to this group or has its origins in a famous victory gained by the British during the American War of Independence is a matter of speculation. There is no doubt whatever, though, that the Malakoff—the semi-circular fortress-like look-out above Pednolva Point—derives from a victory gained by Anglo-French forces in the Crimean War.

Mention of Pednolva brings us back again to names of Cornish origin, which have survived with greatest persistence for local rocks and headlands, largely owing to the strongly traditionalist influence of the fishermen. So we have Carrack Dhu (black rock) near Porthmeor; Bambaluz, Merryn, Browthin, Carnevras, Gowna, Men Derrans, and Men Rousa—all rock names; Carrack Gladden (the rocks on the brink) the bold headland by Carbis Bay; Clodgy Point (a name believed to refer to an old leper settlement there); Lebmas (a fishing ground and headland east of Carrack Gladden) and Scuddy Men, a fishing ground north of St. Ives Head.

Many of the farms in this area also bear ancient Cornish names—indeed, this is the general rule of the district. A glance at the Ordnance Survey map will reveal innumerable examples, some of which are hauntingly beautiful, others weird and strange. A group of remarkable place names comes from the parish of Towednack, to the west of St. Ives, home of many fascinating superstitions. Among these names may be mentioned Skillywadn, Beagletubm, Amalebra, Amalveor, Chylason, Chytodn, Embla, Penderleath, and Trendrine. There is music—and mystery too—in these wonderfully evocative old names which breathe the very spirit of bygone Cornwall.

Readers interested in the history of the mining in the area and in the St Ives artists may like to read:
The St Ives Mining District, Cyril Noall, Dyllansow Truran
Art about St Ives, Roy Ray, Wills Lane Gallery, St Ives